The Foundation
of
Buddhist Meditation

By
Ven. Kalu Rinpoche

LIBRARY OF TIBETAN WORKS AND ARCHIVES

First published in 1973 as a pamphlet
Published in *Four Essential Buddhist Texts* in 1981, 1982
Reprint 1992
Reprint 1998

Cover drawing: Ngawang Choephel

ISBN: 81-85102-61-9

Published by the Library of Tibetan Works and Archives,
Dharamsala, and printed at Indraprastha Press (CBT),
4 Bahadurshah Zafar Marg, New Delhi – 100 002.

Foreword

The Foundation of Buddhist Meditation by Ven. Kalu Rinpoche was first published as a pamphlet by us in 1973. In 1981 it was included in an anthology (*Four Essential Buddhist Texts*) which was reprinted in 1982. Once again we are pleased to offer it independently with minor revisions in response to persistent demand.

The Foundation of Buddhist Meditation outlines the basic meditation practices common to all sects of Tibetan Buddhism.

Ven. Kalu Rinpoche, the present head of the *Shang-pa Kagyu* tradition, is one of Tibet's foremost living meditation masters, and has guided hundreds of disciples through three-year retreats in many countries.

It is hoped that this meditation manual will provide the reader with a deeper insight into the complex scope of Tibetan Buddhist thought and practice.

Gyatsho Tshering
Director, LTWA
December, 1987

Introduction

In this manual, the four teachings which motivate religious practice and the attributes of the Three Jewels are explained. If one completely understands the significance of all these things, one will turn away from the cycle of existence and strive to procure freedom, will believe in action and result (karma), and will either obtain Buddhahood in this life or will become free of this cycle, etc. Moreover when many positive qualities are cultivated, one will consolidate a basis for the holy Dharma. So, please, don't just penetrate the significance of all three things, but, in addition, strive at Dharma practice.

This book, was written by myself, Kalu Rinpoche (Karma Drub-gyud Ten-dzin) for the benefit of all who practice the Dharma. Ken McLoed of Canada did the translation from the Tibetan into English, after which Kungo Losang Lhalungpa checked and corrected the translation manuscript.

May this work deliver many sentient beings from the ocean of suffering, this cycle of existence; may they attain the Castle of Buddha.

Kalu Rinpoche

The Foundation of Buddhist Meditation

by The Very Venerable Kalu Rinpoche

Now in order to embark upon religious practice, right from the start, an awareness of the difficulties of meeting with the opportunities and blessings of this life will anchor the mind and lead one to enter religion; then through the contemplation of impermanence, laziness will be abandoned and one will strive at such practice; belief in seed and results will cause evil to be rejected, virtue to be taken up, and one to act with propriety; and when the misery of the cycle of existence is understood, because of strong revulsion one will want to procure only freedom.

First to possess the eight opportunities means not to be born in the eight unrestful existences which are the hell, preta and animal realms all tormented by suffering exclusively; primitive tribes to which no religion has appeared; the long lived gods adrift on the currents of desire;[1] those human beings who have wrong views, believing neither in religion nor in the law of action and result, those born in a dark aeon when Buddha has not appeared; and those who cannot understand the meaning of religion due to retardation or defects in speech, ears or eyes.

To possess the ten blessings means first to have the five blessings which accrue through oneself; i.e. to obtain the body of a human, to be born in a central country which has religion, to have all five senses intact, to reverse the tide of karma, and to have faith in the Three Jewels; and secondly, to have the five blessings which accrue through others; i.e. the appearance of Buddha, the teaching of religion (Dharma), the stability of the Doctrine, the existence of many who follow the Doctrine, and through the kindness and faith of others to have favorable circumstances for religious practice. Together, the five blessings, from oneself and the five through others comprise the ten blessings. Thus, to possess these, eighteen opportunities and blessings, forms the human birth.

The difficulty of meeting with it is illustrated in three ways: by considering the cause, the numbers, and an example. The karmic cause is the cultivation of a completely pure ethical code. Such individuals are very rare. Number means that while hell beings are as numerous as the dust particles of the earth, pretas as the sand of the Ganges (the sacred river in India), animals as snow flakes, those in the celestial and anti-god realms as the stars at night, those who have a precious human birth with opportunities and blessings are like daytime stars. For example, it is taught that if all the world were water and a wooden yoke were thereupon to be tossed by the winds, and a blind turtle surfaced once every hundred years, for that turtle to put its neck in the yoke would be easier than to obtain the precious human birth.

Thus, at this time when the precious human birth has been obtained, not to set out to follow the path to freedom and so, when completely free from the suffering of the cycle of existence to obtain the permanent peace of Buddhahood, is more wasteful than, for example, a poor man who, finding as many jewels would fill a house, makes no use and so loses them.

So now, resolve to dismiss all worldly work, which is great activity for little purpose, and don't deceive oneself or pretend that one understands Dharma or that one can meditate. Obtain the nectar of religion from a qualified teacher (or spiritual friend), and then after completely comprehending the significance of the Holy Dharma, never depart from the resolution to complete the practice of Dharma by accumulated spiritual merits, eliminating mental impurities, and applying through meditation transformation and spiritual perfection.

Secondly, if impermanence is contemplated, strong clinging to this life diminishes and one is able to cultivate virtue. What is impermanence? All gatherings of riches, enjoyment and splendor are, in the end, dispersed; in the end, buildings ruined; in the end, those who have gathered together are separated; in the end, those born die. Thus every thing is but impermanent.

In addition, the external world which seems solid and firm is impermanent and will be destroyed in stages by fire, water and wind. The force of the coming spring causes the earth to be soft and reddish-brown in colour; trees and plants bring forth shoots and buds. But this is impermanent, for the force of the coming summer causes the earth to be moist and blue-green in color; grass, trees and plants develop leaves and petals. The force of the coming autumn causes the earth to be firm and reddish-yellow in color; grass, trees and plants ripen in fruit. The force of the coming winter causes the earth to be hard and grey in color; grass, trees and plants become dry and brittle; and so on season by season. The sun and moon rising and setting are also impermanent. At day it is clear and bright; at night black and dark. Moreover hours and minutes are impermanent, a passing moment. Impermanent is like a continual water fall: something else similar arises.

All sentient beings,[2] the inner contents of the external world, are impermanent. All those who came before have died, all that are now are dying, all to come will but die. One's self in each year, month, day, hour, and minute draws closer to death. Though brave and greatly courageous, one cannot turn back death; though strong and fleet of foot, there is no freedom in flight; though clever and eloquent, erudite discourse can do nought. Brave troops, sharp weapons, power and influence, clever schemes, wealth or riches, a beautiful girl's body, all these will not turn it away. When the sun goes behind the mountain, there is no one who can possibly delay or detain it.

Nor is this life certain in its length. Death can come in the mother's womb, or at birth, or when one can just begin to crawl or walk, in the time of youth, or after old age: the time of death is not certain. Also there are the causes of death: fire and water, wind and lightning, earthquakes, avalanches, falling houses, weapons, poison, demons, bad food, etc. Which of these causes of death will come is not certain. This life is like a butter lamp in a hurricane, a bubble in water, or a drop of dew on a blade of grass.

There is no yearning for or joy at the coming of death. It is loathed. For, after one has set aside land and house and farm, property and possessions, relatives and close friends, father and mother, children, brother and spouse, together with one's own body, one must go powerless, alone and friendless to an unfamiliar realm, the terrifying Bardo (the stage between death and birth). Since without the slightest exception, the basis for this departure, whether early or late, is part of everything, whenever one sees, hears or thinks of another's death, one must make it part of oneself.

Any man at all who has a sound body, good complexion, and feels happy and comfortable has no thought for death. When the sickness of death strikes, his body's strength ebbs and he cannot even sit in a crouch: the glow of health wanes, and he looks like a corpse; he suffers with no means to prevent the thorns of pain; medicine, rituals, or ceremonies, none of these is of any benefit, and he knows he is to die; his suffering and fear increase and he despairs of leaving everything and having to go alone. As the last meal is taken and the last words are uttered, think, "I also do not pass beyond this nature."

Once death has come, even a person who loved him very much does not want to keep his corpse longer than a day or two; everyone is sickened and looks on in fear. The corpse carriers carry him across the threshold and away to be buried in a cemetery, cremated, hidden in a crevice or given to birds or dogs etc. After all that has taken place, no eyes will ever see him again. Think, "I also will come to the same end."

At that time, the three Precious Jewels[3] and the Lama are the friends who can provide refuge. Since virtue and vice are the only things that bring benefit or harm, strive now towards pure and perfect religious practice.

Since this body is made from the fusion of various parts: black and white karma, secretions from the mother and father, the four elements, space consciousness, etc., and all compounded things are impermanent, so is the body.

In addition, the high become low, the low high, mighty become paupers, poor become rich, enemies change to friends, friends to enemies: in all these changes nothing goes beyond its essential nature of impermanence. So, this holding to the impermanent as permanent is like existing in the delusions of a madman.

This precious human birth now obtained can convey and comprehend ideas, has a full compliment of capabilities, has met spiritual teachers and friends, and has understood the implications of religion. If it should go to waste, even after the sufferings of the cycle have been experienced intensely for a long time, such a foundation as this body may not be obtained again. Thus, since the time one has to live is like the sun peeping through clouds, think about practicing religion completely and vow to do so diligently.

Contemplation of impermanence in this way leads to comprehension of the impermanence of all composite things. Then, manifest attachment to this life decreases, the power of the defilements (desire, aversion, etc.) is destroyed; faith in religion increases, and one works with diligence. He who practices religion is never depressed or weary and will finally realize the meaning of the unborn, undying nature of mind and obtain the perfect accomplishment of the Great Symbol.

Thirdly, it is necessary to cultivate mindfulness of the fallings of the cycle. Although there be death and impermanence, if, like a fire dying or water evaporating, nothing happens afterwards, it would be easy; but mind, whose nature is empty, never dies. The aggregates of mind and body which have come from strong clinging and is the manifestation of delusion breaks up and is dispersed. Then again, from various potentials and causes such as defilements, karma, inclinations, etc., birth takes place wherever appropriate in any of the realms.

The composition of the skandhas[4] incorporates the essential nature of the cycle, i.e. suffering. When there is the existence of the skandhas there is the existence of the potential sorrow that pervades formations; when potential sorrow, through various causes, changes to the feeling of sorrow, it is the sorrow of changes; the sorrow that really is experienced is the sorrow of sorrows. There is no freedom from any of these three sufferings.

Particularly, sentient beings in the six realms experience many different sorrows. First, the beings of the eight hot hells called Reviving, Black Line, Crushing and Destruction, Crying in Agony, Hot, Very Hot, and Worst Torment pass their time only suffering from death, killing, heat and flames. The length of time spent and amount of suffering increase by factors of four from hell. In each of the four directions, there are four other hells called Fire and Hot Mud Trench, Cesspool of Rotting Corpses, Road Full of Razors, and River of Hot Ashes. These hells, situated four in each of four directions of the great hells, make a total of sixteen neighboring hells. There, one is subjected to sufferings suggested by the meaning of the names, and the life span is indefinite. The eight cold hells are called Blistering, Teeth Chattering, Sounding Achoo, Sounding Kyehu, Cracks Like a Flower, Cracks Like a Lotus, and Cracks Like a Large Lotus. In these dwelling places all the mountains and valleys are ice and snow, and it is as cold as can be. The length of time spent in Blistering is given as follows: if from eighty bushels of sesame seeds one seed were removed each year, the time taken to exhaust the seeds would be one lifespan there. The lifespan increases by factors of twenty successively, through the other cold hells, as does the suffering. Finally, the occasional hells may be above or below ground, in indefinite places. Neither the suffering nor lifespan is strictly determined, and the only reason for being there is to suffer.

The pretas: those obscured outwardly do not see a drop of water for twelve years and experience the sorrow of having dry food only. Those inwardly obscured have mouths no larger than the eye of a needle, eyes as thin as a horse's hair, arms and legs like blades of grass, and stomachs as big as mountains, and thus, unable to seek food and drink, experience the sorrow of not putting anything into their mouths and throats. For those obscured in food and drink, food and fluid become filth or molten metal. Those with particular burdens have many pretas living in and eating their bodies and each mother gives birth to five hundred children, etc. Continually subject to the suffering of quarrelling, grabbing, heat, cold, hunger and thirst, they live for five hundred years. One day there is as long as a month for humans.

In the animal realms, there are all those such as nagas,[5] etc., who dwell in seclusion in the ocean or under the ground, and those scattered and living in the places of men: antelopes, carnivores, cows, deer, insects, worms, etc. Size and shape of body and lifespan are uncertain and varied. Foolish and stupid, hungry and thirsty, through heat and cold, frightened and panic-stricken, ever eating one another, they suffer immeasurably. For all nagas, seven times every day usually, scorching sand falls like rain and flays the flesh to the bone. Fear of garuda birds constantly plagues them. All those animals which one can see with one's own eyes, when examined accurately, will be seen to have sorrows which seem in-exhaustible. On top of this great suffering, they become subject to desire and attachments and the other defilements, and commit various unwholesome acts, such as killing, etc. Since they all neither know nor recall even a vestige of the root of virtue, i.e. faith, compassion, etc., one should have compassion and strive at the means to avoid birth there. These are the circumstances of the three lower realms.

Of the three higher realms and their circumstances, the

first to be explained is that of humans. There are four great sorrows: birth, old age, sickness and death.

First is the suffering of birth. After the previous body has been cast aside, in the imagined Bardo body one passes the time powerless, in fear and in pain. According to the amount of merit previously accumulated, one sees from afar a beautiful house, or a hut of grass or leaves or a crack in a wall, and rushes there. According to whether one is to be born male or female, one feels attachment and aversion to the mother and father. Then the secretions of the mother and fluid from the father and one's own consciousness are mixed. At that time, all conscious memory is jumbled like the unclear dreams of a thick sleep.

In the first week in the mother's womb, the suffering is like being roasted or fried on hot copper. At that time, the appearance is of soft rice; this stage is named Mer Mer. In the second week, the All-Touching Wind causes the four elements to manifest and the appearance is like cold butter and is call Nur Nur. In the third week, the Storing Up Wind causes the four elements to manifest strongly; now the shape is like an insect and is called Tar Tar. And so, similar changes take place stage by stage until the seventh week when the Twisting Wind gives rise to the four arms and legs; the suffering is like having the limbs pulled out by a strong person and being spread out by a stick. By stages, the shape forms and sorrows come; in the eighth week, the Hole Forming Wind comes and the nine orifices form; there is the additional suffering as if a finger were probing an open wound.

When the mother takes something cold, there is suffering like being immersed in ice; when she eats a great deal, the suffering is like being crushed by boulders; if only a little is eaten, then like hanging in the air, when running or being very active, like rolling down into a large abyss; and when she has intercourse, it is like being pierced by iron needles.

In the thirty-seventh week after entering the womb, there is the recognition that the womb is really like a jail:

dark and smelly and filthy, and completely depressing, inducing the desire to escape. In the thirty-eighth week, one is moved in the direction of the gate of birth by the Flower Gathering Wind, at which time there is suffering like being spun on an iron wheel. So, from the first moment of conception in the womb, one was cooked as if in molten copper, disturbed by twenty-eight different winds, and was stewed in the gravy of the mother's blood, until the body was completely finished. Now, the Mouth Down Wind turns the body upside down, the hands stretch out, and out one comes. At this time, the suffering is like being pulled through a net of iron. When born, at the time of coming out there is the sorrow of being thrown into the centre of life. At later times, various sorrows such as the skin being flayed (when first washed) will come. If these sorrows are thought about, is there anyone who thinks he is willing to enter the womb again?

The sufferings of old age, also, are immeasurable. Where as the body was straight and firm before, now it changes to being bent and stooped and needs a cane for support; the hair changes in color; the face, etc., is no longer beautiful; the skin which was fine and soft like Chinese silk becomes a thick heap of wrinkles, just as a freshly blooming lotus is white and red but when old becomes dry, wrinkled and shrivelled. The lift of the body is broken; both sitting and moving are wearisome; the power of the mind is destroyed; and there is little inclination to do anything. The capabilities of the sense exhausted; the eyes no longer see forms clearly, the ears don't hear sounds, the nose doesn't sense odors, the tongue doesn't taste flavors, the touch of the body has little pleasure and mentally, memories are unclear, now remembered, now forgotten. Because everything is disordered and chaotic, one is unhappy and contemptuous. The wealth gathered before is exhausted and there is much suffering from being powerless, etc. Thus, one is very depressed. After one sees clearly that there is nothing else but death, one has to sit with the head bent down in sadness. When the present time passes, the end of life is reached. The breath, moving in and out, causes a rasping sound. Composite things that age together decay together.

The sufferings of disease are: one can't bear the ravages of fever, nor can one lie in the sick bed; the lower half of the body can't bear the upper, there is no wish to eat or drink nor power to do what one wants; one is dependent on doctors; property and wealth are exhausted; one has to be carefully examined; even if the day passes, there is still the night, etc. The time is passed in such suffering.

The suffering of death: for all ordinary mortals, as soon as they come to the great crossroads on the road of the cycle, the sickness of death strikes; they are cut off and divorced from happiness and tormented by disease; the mouth is parched; what is familiar changes; legs and arms thrash about and one trembles uncontrollably; spittle, mucous, urine and stools defile the body; one breathes hoarsely; the doctors give up; all means are exhausted; strong and violent delusions arouse fear and panic; the movement of breath ceases; mouth and nose gape open. This world is cast aside, the great change comes, and one moves to another realm, enters into great darkness, falls into a great abyss, is carried away by a great ocean, is chased by the winds of karma, and wanders with no fixed aim. House, farm, fields, jewels, wealth, property, fortune, power and spouse, together with the body so dear: all are set aside.

With tears trickling at the time of departure, first earth is absorbed into water and the trembling body feels as if a mountain were relentlessly crushing it. Then water is absorbed into fire, and fluid dribbles uncontrollably from the mouth, nose and so forth; one feels that one is being carried away in flood. As fire dissolves into wind, the mouth and nose become dry and the eyes turn upward; body heat begins to leave the limbs and it is as if there were a great fire roaring and burning inside oneself. As wind dissolves into consciousness the breath stops and a great wind, gisting and whining, is felt with great apprehension and fear. Then when consciousness, is absorbed into ignorance, white brilliance, then red and then black are perceived; all mental activity ceases and one becomes oblivious. After a period of between three and four days, mental activity is revived and the various manifestations of the Bardo arise. Once again, the force of karma brings birth in the appropriate place in the six realms.

However, these four great sufferings are not the only ones. There are also other sorrows. One sometimes has to be separated from those one loves dearly, one's parents, brothers, spouse, etc., even when living; also, one is completely separated from them by death. There are no means to forget this sorrow. Then, the suffering caused by meeting angry enemies or being beaten, defeated, killed, struck, and abused by poisons one to the point of not eating at day nor sleeping at night. Also there are the sorrows of seeking but not finding what one doesn't have and the sorrow of being unable to keep what one does have. Especially, in these degenerate times one has to spend all the time, day and night, suffering from anxiety, depression, attachment, and aversion.

Thus, be ever mindful of the failings of desire's yearnings, and know that all the dharmas[6] of the cycle of existence are at no time still, just like ripples on water; that it's as if there were nothing, but delusions appearing like magic, or like dreams. If revulsion (for existence) and contentment (with one's material situation) arise, one will be able to sit quietly with the mind happy and at ease.

The sufferings of the titans are: although equal to the gods in riches and possessions, generally, the force of jealousy causes them to quarrel with outsiders, insiders, with everyone, and there is especially violent suffering from quarrelling with the gods.

In the desire realm, gods suffer from quarrelling with the titans, from not satisfying the yearnings of desire, and from death and banishment. At death, five signs appear: the god's clothes become smelly, his garland and flowers wilt, perspiration breaks out from his armpits, his body begins to smell, and his seat becomes uncomfortable. All the other gods and goddesses run away, and dying by himself, he suffers greatly and is panic-stricken, seeing the place of his next birth. He must experience these sorrows for seven days. Although in the form and formless realms there are no sufferings like these, because death does come and one has no power to stay, there is the sorrow of fetching a worse situation.

So, since hell beings suffer from heat and cold, pretas from hunger and thirst, and animals from stupidity, foolishness and eating each other, and humans suffer from birth, old age, sickness, and death, titans from quarrelling and gods from death and their subsequent fall; one must strive to be free from sinking into the cycle of the ocean of suffering, and to attain the blissful, sacred, and perfect Buddhahood.

Fourthly, one must understand karmic cause and result. Now the subjection to the various manifestations of delusions of comfort and discomfort in the six worlds and the three realms[7] arises through the power of karma. First, non-meritorious actions are the ten vices, etc., which originate from a defiled mind. The ten vices are given as follows.

Through the gate of the body, there is taking life. Taking life out of desire means killing for the sake of meat, skin, bones, musk, etc., or for money, or to protect oneself or one's friends; out of anger means that which is done in enmity or quarrelling; and to take life for offering or gifts, thinking it is virtuous or the like, is to kill from stupidity. From these actions, the completely developed result is birth as a sentient being in hell; if born as a human, the result which corresponds with the cause of the act is that one likes to take life; the result that agrees with the experience is that one will have a short life and much sickness and, for a long succession of lives, one will have to face being killed; the result in environment is that one is born in a rocky and steep land where there is much danger for life. Secondly, there is taking that which is not given; stealing forcefully and violently with little provocation; clandestine stealing without being seen; and stealing deceptively in contracts, measures or by cheating. The various results successively are birth in the pretas; if born as a human, to be poor and unhappy, to like to steal, and to be born in a country with much snow and hail. Thirdly, there are wrong desires which means copulation when forbidden by relationship, i.e. with one's mother, sister, or daughter; when forbidden by commitment, i.e. another man's wife, or concubines of another man or king, etc.; or when forbidden by religion, i.e. not even with one's wife in the vicinity of a Lama, in a temple, near a stupa, in a place where many are gathered, when observing a temporary vow of chastity, or when one's wife is pregnant. The four results are birth in the pretas; one's spouse is unattractive and quarrelsome like an enemy; one is always dissatisfied with one's own spouse and constantly thinks of others; and the country of birth is very dusty.

Through the door of speech: first there is lying. The various kinds are lying about one's spiritual attainments, lying to cause harm, and telling ordinary lies. The four results are to be born in the animal realm; if born as a human, to receive much slander, to have halitosis, to like to lie, and to be born in a country that is high and low, and hot and cold. Creating disharmony means to cause two people to disagree in the presence of each other, to cause a split by speaking indirectly, and to cause a split subversively when they are separated. The results, successively, are birth among hell beings; if born as a human, to be divorced from companionship, to like schisms, and to be born in a country that is steep and precipitous. Harsh language entails speaking viciously to another, to slander in various ways through jokes and jests, and to speak vilely of another to his friends and those near to him. The results, again, are birth in hell; and if born as a human, to hear various unpleasant words and sounds, to always like evil speech, and to be born where the land is hot and dry, with crags, ravines and brambles.

Idle talk means to repeat mantras wrongly, to explain scriptures incorrectly, to talk a lot with no purpose, and to explain religion to those who have no respect for it. The results, successively, are to be born as an animal; and if born as a human, no one enjoys one's speech, one's speech is ignoble, and one is born where summer and winter are confused.

Then there are the vices of mind. Coveting includes being so very attached to one's ancestry, body, character, wealth or possessions that one thinks that should they grace another, it would not be right; or thinking that what is under another's control should be under one's own. The results, successively, are to be born in the pretas; if born as a human, not to accomplish what one thinks of, to have great desire, and to be born in a country where crops grow badly. Ill-will means to be so angry as to fight or go to war with another; to think meanly from jealousy, or to think of harming someone out of enmity. The results, again, are birth in the hells; and if born as a human, to be angry in nature, to be treated as an enemy for no reason, and to be born in a country that is harsh, mountainous and cut with deep gorges. Wrong views consist of holding the opinion that there is no truth in action and result, that the relative and ultimate truths are wrong, or that Holy Ones are imperfect. Again the results are birth as an animal; and if born as a human, to be so stupid that one understands nothing, to have no inclination whatsoever for studying and to be born in a poor and barren country.

The very worst acts among the ten vices are: to take the life of one's father, or spiritual teacher; to take ungiven wealth from the Three Jewels; through seduction to cause another to break vows of chastity or celibacy; to deceive a lama through lies; to belittle the One-Thus-Gone (Tathagata); to cauuse disharmony among the congregation of monks or religious friends; to speak harshly to one's mother, father, or an awakened saint; through idle talk to cause one who wishes to practice religion to wander; to covet precious objects which are consecrated to the Three Jewels; to engender ill-will potent enough to commit inexpiable action; and to have wrong views from holding conflicting opinions.

If the defilements are considered, anger, greed stupidity, desire, jealousy and pride lead to birth as a hell-being, preta, animal, man, titan, and god respectively. Committing many bad actions leads to birth as a hell-being; committing a moderate number, birth as a preta; and a few as an animal. Good and bad actions mixed together lead to the multifarious lives of the three higher realms, i.e. as human and celestial beings. Accordingly, as the one transgressed against is high, low, or in-between in station, one is born as a hell-being, animal, or preta respectively. It is taught that as long as these evil acts are not abandoned, they grow ever larger.

Secondly, as for meritorious karma, it arises from the components of virtue, unattached love, a helping mind, small wants, contentment, etc. When taking life is abandoned, and life protected, the completely ripened result is birth as a god; and, if and when born as a human, one's life is long and free from sickness, one is rich and for oceans of lives will be happy and joyful with little thought for killing; when attachment to one's country is abandoned, and one is generous, the power of king, etc., will be accumulated; even if born as an ordinary human, one will have the very best wealth and possessions, will take joy in giving, and will be born in a country with the best in food and riches. When wrong desires are abandoned, and morals are protected, the results are to be born among celestial beings; and if and when born as a human, to have a fine, beautiful spouse with whom one is in accord, to have contentment in continual friendship, and to be in a country both pleasant and comfortable.

As for speech, when lies are abandoned and truth is spoken the results are to be born among gods or men, to have everyone regard one's words as true, to like to give honest views, and to be in a level country where fruit is always ripening. When creating disharmony is given up and one is the agent for reconciliation, the results are birth among gods or men, everything spoken will be regarded as true and will please everyone, and one will always like agreement; the country will have little hail or sleet, and food and wealth will be easily found when sought. When harsh language is abandoned and one speaks softly or gently, the results are to be born among gods or men, to rest in everyone's praise and to hear pleasing speech, to enjoy gentle talk, and to be born in a gentle country moderate in temperature. When idle talk is abandoned and one bears only meaningful news, the results are birth among men, one's words are noble and pleasing to others, one is happy with little talking and the country is even in terrain and climate.

When covetousness is abandoned and there is contentment and few wants, the results are birth among gods and men, to be born happy and to accomplish whatever one thinks of, to be always content with one's possessions, and to be born in a pleasant place. When ill-will is abandoned and one has a helpful mind, the results are to be born among gods or men, to be loved by all, to accomplish any purpose that one wishes, to desire to help sentient beings, and to be born in a country where whatever is needed or wanted comes. When wrong views are abandoned, one is born among gods or men, is venerated and inherits the best intelligence and wisdom, enjoys striving at studying and is born in a country with fertile land and wholesome food.

Thirdly, the karma of stillness: when the seed is the practice of concentration in meditative trances, the result obtained is birth in such a state. Generally, these trances are based on the practice of the ten virtuous deeds. From that overall background, there are eight preparations which precede the actual concentration, and when at various times in the trance, examination, investigation, joy, and bliss are all present, the first stage of absorption has been achieved. When in the actual practice, there is no examination or investigation, yet joy or bliss, the second absorption is reached. When joy ceases and there is just bliss, the third absorption is reached and when all four cease, the fourth is reached. When the absorption deepens beyond these four, one experiences the Infinity of Space. If this absorption is practiced, one is born in the perception of the Infinity of Space. Beyond this absorption, there are the perceptions of the Infinity of Consciousness, Nothingness and Peak of Cyclic Existence. In this state the subtle discrimination is neither there nor not there, and one can be born as celestial beings in these states of perception.

As the mind arrives on each succeeding level, there is successively more separation from attachment; thus mind becomes detached and penetrates to the next stage. All these eight trances consist of a one-pointed virtuous mind.

Accordingly, the agent which produces the substance of Samsara is no other than these three types of sullied karma.

In brief, in the cycle of existence the root is ignorance from which arises the clinging to duality; then from discriminating consciousness on the one hand come the defilements, from awareness on the other come wisdom, faith compassion and a helpful disposition. From good or bad karma come the results of the higher and lower realms and their corresponding happiness, and suffering. When the good and bad karma is mixed, various, uncertain sorrows and comforts are experienced. All the varied karma makes the multiplicity of these beings, since from differing actions different results will come.

Even though this life is generated as the karmic result of virtue which was practiced in the immediately preceding life, this life may pass in misery because of other karmic conditions such as stealing from others in a past life: for example, one would have to be born as a poorman. Even though this life is generated as the karmic result of evil practiced in the immediately preceding life, this life may pass in great prosperity because of other karmic conditions, such, as generosity in previous lives: an example would be a rich serpent-god (naga). If both generative karma and overall karmic conditions are virtuous, the birth might be such as a Universal Monarch; if both are evil, then as a hell being.

Present karma whose results are experienced in this very life are such as: inexpiable action prepared and executed in reference to a Buddha (or Enlightened Sage), for instance, by Lha Jin[8] who experienced the fires of hell in this life; or it refers to pure thought and object such as the man and wife who gave Sariputra a meal and later harvested ears of corn of gold. Some results are called 'Those To Be Experienced After Birth': these include the five inexpiable and the five nearly inexpiable actions,[9] whose results will be experienced immediately after this life. Those to be experienced at another time will be experienced in three or four later births, whenever they come.

One may accumulate karma through actions which would be like worshipping the Jewels through faith, or killing a man from anger. Or one may accumulate karma with no actions, such as rejoicing in the bad or good actions of others. Or one may not gather anything through one's actions such as sitting down to meditate but letting the mind wander.

Black thought joined to white action would be like erecting a monastery or stupa for the sake of fame, etc. White thought joined with black action would be like speaking roughly or beating and striking someone in order to help him.

Collective karma is the accumulation of similar karma and so produces similar results, i.e. all sentient beings perceive the universe the same way. Particular karma will be experienced from the karma of each individual sentient being and is the varied experience of happiness and sorrow because of differences in individual environment, bodies and possessions. Since after the results from white karma are finished, the results from black are experienced, happiness in early life may turn to misery in later life.

While protecting life results in long life, striking and beating causes much sickness. Through generosity, one comes to have great possessions, but when the mind is full of harm, one will have many enemies. Although one may find a beautiful, perfect spouse as a result of abandoning adultery, disharmony created in one's past life results in discord. Those who abandon harsh language will be loved by all; those who covet will always be destitute. Although one is born in a home with wealthy parents from having made offerings and being generous, jealousy of other's generosity results in oneself becoming destitute in this life. The results of smaller generosity have led to birth in a poor household, but through service to all one's elders and parents, etc., one becomes respected and is praised and revered by all. Although born rich because of previous generosity, etc., not liking religion results in becoming one with wrong views. Although previously one may have very powerfully practiced virtue, i.e. making offerings, gifts, etc., the power of jealously or other defilements distorts prayers; and while the birth is one joined to great power, one perpetrates unwholesome karma very powerfully. Although previous virtuous karma may be small, when one stands fast with faith at death, one is born into a religious home. When previously one practiced religion out of faith and compassion, at the present time family, body and possessions are the very best, religion is similarly practiced, and one travels onwards on the path to enlightenment.

If one comes to believe in the inevitable results of interdependence and cause and effect, then indeed one has penetrated to the centre of the root of the teaching of Buddha.

Revulsion at the cycle and the urge to procure freedom are like the root of a tree; faith with compassion is like the trunk; practice of virtue and abandonment of unwholesome action are the branches; the levels are virtues beyond limit; the flowers are in possession of the essence of transformation and perfection (according to esoteric teachings); and the fruit is the attainment of the Castle of Full Enlightenment, Buddha.

When one has become disgusted with the cycle of existence (Samsara), how does one practice religion? First, when one knows the attributes of the Rare Jewels, one goes for refuge and then learns the reason for clearing away obscurations[10] and gathering accumulations of spiritual merits through one's devotion, etc. If one does not know the reason for wanting to practice religion, the methods of practice or the results of religious practice, it would be like shooting an arrow in a black fog.

Therefore, The Awakened One (Buddha), as a sentient being first produced the Thought of Enlightenment (Bodhichitta); and then for three immeasurable aeons gathered spiritual merits, cleared obscuration away, perfected enlightened deeds as vast as an ocean, and when the five paths and ten stages were crossed, he attained Completely Perfected Awakening Enlightenment. Now, the real nature of Awakening is to possess three qualities: the great cessation which is the complete removal of the two obscurations together with their associated habits; the great realization of awareness which is an accurate seeing, not confused by all the phenomena of discrimination; and the great brave mind which is activity arising continually and pervasively from spontaneous compassion for the benefit of beings.

When the meanings are considered after the awakening from the sleep-like ignorance, mind is enlightened in the two knowledges of knowing how everything appears; this state is called Awakened Enlightenment (Buddha).

Each cause has its own result. Through the possession of the Compassionate Thought and from the successive perfection of both the accumulations which are gathered by performing the six perfections, the twin manifestations of Enlightenment are obtained. Moreover, when all karma is accumulated through actions powered by compassion for those lower and by faith in sacred objects, merit is gathered whose result when completely ripened is the accomplishment of two form manifestations. Through the practice of absorption in meditation devoid of conceptualization, wisdom is accumulated and the flawless result is the accomplishment of the Body of Dharma.

The omnipresent Body of Dharma pervades all Samsara and Nirvana, is beyond all intellectual postulation, and is devoid of arising, existence, and cessation.

In the Jogmin-gyi Shing[11] Buddha Field beyond the three realms, the Perfect Manifestation Body arises before all the tenth level Bodhisattvas.[12] This gathering of the Buddha's own appearance and the appearance of the Bodhisattvas is called the Mutual Manifestation Body.

Subduing beings with exposition on various arts and science is the Skillful Emanation. Subduing beings in various forms such as a king and a deer, etc., is the Bodily Emanation. Through the twelve great deeds, benefit for all sentient beings is administered by the Perfect Emanation.

Thus, the twin form manifestations manifest from previous aspiration and invocation for manifestation, in order to help train beings, form the innate power and blessings of the Dharma Body.

In their distinctive manifestations, the Dharma Body appears when the obscurations of inaccurate knowledged are cleared away; the Manifestation Body by clearing away the obscurations of defilements; and the Emanation Body by the clearing away of the obscurations of karma.

In the great awareness of Buddha, there is not any Dharma in Samsara, Nirvana or the path that is not known or seen. It is as if everything were placed in the palm of the hand. The karma of the three times, the past, present and future, the seeds of karma, the result of karma—everything is known individually, unconfusedly, and clearly without any obscuration. This is the Awareness of Knowledge. Great spontaneous love going out to all beings without discrimination with regard to distance or association with a ceaseless flow of kindness is loving-kindness and compassion. Functioning which never ceases and brooks no interruption, though functioning in different ways according to the potential of individuals having conducive or adverse relations, yet opens the doors to temporal benefit to the higher realms and then to final freedom, and continues to arise until all of

the cycle that exists is emptied is called deeds and functioning.

With the power of inspiration and blessings of the above,
a sentient being, through the successive arising of faith,
devotion, respect, love and compassion, and understanding
that all dharmas (subjective and objective phenomena) are
empty in reality and realizing that they are like magic,
destroys all clinging to the reality of Samsara. Absorbed
completely in Peaceful Tranquility and Insight, and crossing
the Five Paths and Ten Stages with the six and ten perfections, he is protected from the great fear and sufferings of
the cycle of existence and guided to ultimate Enlightenment. This is the capability of refuge from the power of
Samsara.

Thus, the all-knowing awareness, loving kindness and
compassion, deeds and functioning, and power and capability for protection are the supreme qualities of Awakened
Enlightenment.

Now, those who have arrived at the eighth up to the
tenth levels possess ten powers: the power of life, which is
the ability to obtain and stay in any existence at will; the
power of mind, which is the ability to be absorbed exactly in
whatever state of meditation is desired; the power of neces-
sities which is the ability to rain down riches and jewels and
food for all sentient beings; the power over karma, which is
the ability to inspire others to cultivate good karma which
will be experienced at another time; the power of birth,
which is the ability to be born in the desire realm without
getting stained by impurities by staying in meditation; the
power of creation, which is the ability to change any of the
four elements at will; the power of miracles, which is the
ability to demonstrate innumerable miracles for the benefit
of sentient beings; the power of wisdom, which is to know
completely the true significance of all dharma (phenomena);
and the power of Dharma, which is the ability to satisfy
completely the minds of sentient beings of different tongues
and different capabilities by explaining the Dharma in its

assembly of words and phrases in one single exposition. With respect to these powers, Buddhas are much greater and more sacred.

In addition, the thirty-two major perfections and eighty minor perfections of the body, sixty special tones of harmonious speech, ten forces, four grounds for no fear, eighteen differences, etc,. and all the distinct and completely ripened attributes number over a million. If through some inconceivably great miracle the form were seen, there would be no disagreement. Such is Precious Rare Awakened Enlightenment (Buddha).

Speech, hidden and unencompassable by thought, with pure melody rains down the Dharma of the various vehicles, Great and Small, according to faith, capability and realm, simultaneously on gods, nagas, and men, both kind and mean, and animals, etc., in their own respective tongues. Moreover, even though speaking to every stream of being which is to be trained in places both near and far, the quality of the sound is perfectly suited, is lacking in all faults such as speaking too quickly, stuttering, halting, etc., and is soft, gentle and melodious. In all the Buddha realms, the other worlds, and other realms, until all of Samsara is emptied, the Dharma, noble in the beginning, middle and end, deep and extensive, works for the benefit of beings. Such is the Precious Rare Dharma.

Then, all who have practiced the Dharma the best of all speech successively: Sravkas, Pratyekas, Arhants[13] and all those on the spiritual stages from the first to the tenth and final comprise the Transcendent Sangha. The Sangha of individuals consists of all those who abide in any of the three vows: ordination, Bodhisattva, or Vajrayana, whichever is applicable. Such is the Precious Rare Sangha.

Thus one should go for refuge in the knowledge that Buddha is the permanent refuge, Dharma the path, and Sangha the companions.

From the play of the discipline of Buddha, the Accomplished Conqueror beyond sorrow, who is the very self of the five wisdoms and three bodies, arise the assembly of deities, the Yidams, roots of attainment. He who bestows the pith of the yogas of Transformation and Perfection of these Yidams at every stage of ripening, liberation, and final attainment is the Lama, root of all blessings. Depending on that practice all actions, pacifying, extending, influencing, and subduing are accomplished with the support of Dakinis and Defenders of the Dharma, the roots of all activity. These are the three roots.

The seekers of refuge are oneself and all sentient beings. The objects in which refuge is sought are all of the above. The real reason for refuge is to seek refuge from the eight and sixteen fears, and ultimately from the sorrow of the lower realms and the cycle (from now until the moment of enlightenment). To go for refuge, understanding these three things is the root of the religion of Buddha.

If one goes for refuge in Buddha with clear faith, believing in and wanting to reach Buddha, one believes the Dharma that he taught. To practice its methods and to take it to heart is to go for refuge in Dharma. By listening to the speech of all the Awakened Ones and individuals who have studied the meaning of the Dharma and to practice and follow in their path is to go for refuge in the Sangha. If one goes for refuge in such a way, Buddha decreed that in every life, both this and later, one will travel the path of freedom, one will meet the precious Doctrine of Buddha and will not encounter evil companions and will not stay in thought and action; nor will obstacles cause one to stumble, one will not be born in lower realms, and with all vehicles having a foundation, the cycle of existence will come to an end.

Thus, imagine that all the deities of the Three Jewels and Three Roots are really gathered in the sky, radiant with brilliant light, and with devotion prostrate before them with body, speech and mind; offer everything substantial and imaginable that is beautiful or pleasing in form, sound, smell, taste, and touch. With extreme regret confess all the obscuring unwholesome acts that have been accumulated from the time that has no beginning, and vow not to commit them in the future.

These are blessings which all these objects of refuge have; in mind, the very being of knowledge, love and capability; in speech, secret and inconceivable; in body, great merit and inconceivable qualities. With all these and one's own great faith, devotion, and inner thought, the basis and interdependence of all the truths of the arising of conditions and of emptiness, i.e. that all dharmas are by their essential nature non-demonstrable fall together. Then as all fog-like obscurations and unwholesome acts are thinned out and purified, there is Awakening; and as the accumulation of merit and wisdom rise bit by bit, like the sun, the wisdom of knowledge of all that is and the way it is, Enlightens; thus, the Enlightened State of Buddha, Awakened Enlightenment, is attained. Until then, during the intervening lives, all the happiness of the higher realms is experienced, as excellent fruit and grain grows from sound roots and stalks. To go for refuge with great faith and to clear away obscurations and to gather accumulations are extremely important. Have great faith in the Sakya, Gelug, Kagyu and Nyingma schools, since all are exactly the means of liberating all sentient beings from Samsara by training them all in the religion of Awakened Enlightenment.

For the substance of the practice of religion, one of the middle capability practices virtue, abandons wrong action and consolidates the five foundations which are each practiced one hundred thousand times. Then, one trains the mind in concentration and purification, and sets out to meditate and realize a Yidam; and then meditates on the Six Yogas, especially Heat Yoga. By gaining mastery over vase like energy through four practices and with various exercises, and through the projection, retention, distribution, and scattering of vital fluids, mind and body become full of bliss; the unity of warmth and blissful emptiness, i.e. the Great Symbol (Mahamudra) is realized. Someone of the highest capabilities, when ripened in his stream of being by initiation, immediately after the explanation of Mahamudra or perfection, meditates and will cross decisively the various paths and stages.

Now if one is able to comprehend well the meaning of all these teachings, one will turn away from clinging to the cycle, and the resolve to peruse the benefits of freedom will be born. Faith will be born from an understanding of the qualities of the Precious Rare Ones, and compassion will arise for all suffering sentient beings. Then, if one devotes to a Lama, and after seeking the key instruction, meditates, one will definitely come to obtain both ordinary and perfect attainments.

NOTES

1. The three higher births are birth as a human, as a titan or as a god (or celestial being).
2. Sentient being refers to any being that possesses mind: i.e. a hell being, preta, animal, human, titan, or god.
3. The three Precious Jewels are the Buddha, the Dharma and the Sangha. These will be discussed later.
4. Skandha is a Sanskrit word meaning heap or pile. A sentient being may be viewed as a heap of forms, feelings, cognitions, volitions, and consciousness.
5. Nagas are a class of animals that might be termed serpent-gods, since they have a serpent like body, but may be very powerful or rich.
6. Dharma, in this context, refers to all subjective and objective phenomena.
7. The six worlds are as in note 2. The three realms are the desire realm (from the hell beings up to and including the first level of gods), the form realm (the next seventeen levels of gods), and the formless realm (the last four levels).
8. Lha Jin, or Devadatta, was Buddha Shakyamuni's cousin. Somewhat envious of Buddha's station, he tried to harm Buddha on a number of occasions. On one occasion, he succeeded in hurting Buddha with a stone. As a result, he came to suffer extreme agony later in his life.
9. The five inexpiable acts are: to kill one's mother, father spiritual teacher, or a saint, or to harm a Buddha. The five nearly inexpiable acts are: to kill a novice or full monk, to bring down a nun, mutilate an image of Buddha or scriptures, and to destroy a temple or shrine.
10. Obscurations are mental impurities that hide the true nature of mind (ignorance), from passions, and from karma.
11. Jogmin-gyi-Shing is the Buddha field of the celestial Buddha Vajradhara (Dorje Chang).
12. Bodhisattvas are Awakened Saints who pursue enlightenment in order to liberate all sentient beings from sorrow. The ten levels of Bodhisattvas reflect the degree of realization of enlightenment attained.
13. These are various classes of accomplished spiritual beings.